YOUR KNOWLEDGE HAS VALUE

AF140795

- We will publish your bachelor's and master's thesis, essays and papers

- Your own eBook and book - sold worldwide in all relevant shops

- Earn money with each sale

Upload your text at www.GRIN.com and publish for free

Bibliographic information published by the German National Library:

The German National Library lists this publication in the National Bibliography; detailed bibliographic data are available on the Internet at http://dnb.dnb.de .

Imprint:

Copyright © 2010 GRIN Verlag, Open Publishing GmbH
Print and binding: Books on Demand GmbH, Norderstedt Germany
ISBN: 978-3-668-16143-6

This book at GRIN:

http://www.grin.com/en/e-book/316590/nordic-societies-and-cultures-a-lecture-diary

Hanna Wilkes

Nordic Societies and Cultures. A Lecture Diary

GRIN Publishing

GRIN - Your knowledge has value

Since its foundation in 1998, GRIN has specialized in publishing academic texts by students, college teachers and other academics as e-book and printed book. The website www.grin.com is an ideal platform for presenting term papers, final papers, scientific essays, dissertations and specialist books.

Visit us on the internet:

http://www.grin.com/

http://www.facebook.com/grincom

http://www.twitter.com/grin_com

Contents

I – 14.9.2010: Nordic co-operation and Nordic identity

The idea of creating a Scandinavian nation occurred in the nineteenth century and had been a pan-national movement during the European building process. Sweden, Norway and Denmark wanted to incorporate to strengthen their power because they were small states with little military power and still weakened by lossy wars. Their union should be strong enough to be capable of challenging Russia or Prussia and Germany. Another aim was to create a common cultural heritage. Furthermore, the relationship between the former enemies Sweden and Denmark should grow up to a peaceful one. A starting point for such a positive relation and also for the Scandinavianism had been the crowning of a Danish writer by the Swedish. Sweden-Norway had already been in a common union, both were governed by the same Swedish king. In the beginnings, Finland had not been included in these plans for a Scandinavian nation.

Scandinavianism had mainly been Swedish and Danish. The political idea was to found a united kingdom under Swedish rule but there were also cultural plans. Besides a common cultural identity, liberal political values should be included.

The idea of Scandinavianism had never been realized. When in 1853 it became clear that war breaks out between Russia and Western countries, Sweden became pro-Western whereas Denmark got pro-Russian. Moreover, there were growing tensions between the union Sweden-Norway. These are two examples for too many and not only political disagreements between the three nations so that the plan of a union finally failed.

Nevertheless, nothing had been in vain. Due to the activeness of the Nordic countries to realize the Scandinavianism, a basic for other Nordic co-operations had been built up. Since 1945, after World War II, the need to strengthen the Nordic block had become primary. Meanwhile Finland had also been included in plans concerning Scandinavia. After its independence from Russia in 1917/18, it orientated itself towards the other Nordic countries. Therefore, the Nordic Council had been established which brought along a Nordic passport union, a common labour market and the Nordic social insurance convention.

The Nordic Council is a discussion forum meeting once a year whereas the venue and the presidency change regularly. Its aim is to run several projects for example in the fields of culture, economy, environment or education. This institution is financed by the Nordic countries.

At the end of the lesson we discussed following question: *What if the idea about Scandinavianism had been realized?*

I assume that such a union would not have lasted for a long time. The Nordic Council is indeed a corporation between the Scandinavian countries yet I understand the Scandinavianism as a union that should have been much stronger and engaging than this council. The aims and visions of three nations had probably not been compatible for a long time.

However, if this idea really had been worked out, I guess Finland, Sweden and Denmark would not have joined the European Union. Their own common union would be enough. In addition, I suppose that the Finnish language would have changed so that it would be more related to the Swedish or Danish language.

II – 16.9.2010: The Nordic Welfare State model

The welfare systems in the Scandinavian countries are the most extensive ones in the world. They head regularly the surveys and comparisons based on topics such as health, life expectation or social equality. After Gøsta Esping-Andersen there are three classifications of welfare regimes, the so called *Three Worlds of Welfare Capitalism*.

1. **The liberal model (e.g. USA):** It is a means-tested welfare system that should be seen as a basic safety net. Small benefits are only provided for the poorest people.

2. **The continental (conservative) model (e.g. Germany):** It is also a means-tested system, though the benefits are more generous. The benefits depend on the social status of a citizen.

3. **The social democratic model (e.g. Finland):** There are universal benefits for everyone whereas these ones are not just hard cash but also services.

Because of the widespread services the Nordic countries offer their inhabitants they belong to the third category. This model of a welfare state has become a part of the national identity of the Scandinavians. People believe in the image of *The Good State* which means that they consider the state as a positive institution and as reliable. Moreover, the state is supposed to guarantee the freedom and liberty of every individual. This trust is a requirement for such a model to run.

Yet what is the idea behind universal benefit? The answer is simple: If everyone receives money from the state, nobody complains about high taxes. And these are another trait of the social democratic system.

In the Nordic Welfare State model the focus of the benefit is on the individual and on the state. The family does not play such a big role like in Germany or in the USA.

Another main feature is the topic *gender equality*. Nordic countries have one of the highest female labour force rates due to the fact that the family and children policy had been improved. Nevertheless, the labour market is still gender divided and there are also inequalities in the salaries between men and women.

The name of the third category already leads to the assumption that the Social Democrats had created this kind of a model. Indeed this party had an important influence on the Nordic states and their history. Anyway, it is not correct to maintain that the Nordic welfare state was its creation. Lots of features already existed before the Social Democrats were established.

At the moment, this until now well working welfare system is faced with some problems. There are ideological crises and also economical-structural ones. Some say that in consequence of the globalization and the mass immigration the system gets to stumble. Others presume that the Nordic State Welfare model had just been a project with a beginning and also an end.

This topic was interesting for me because in the last semester at my home university I visited a course titled *comparative cultural studies: USA* in which I learned a lot about the American mentality and also about their welfare system.

Among the basic traditional values of American people there are for example individual freedom, equality of opportunity and self-reliance. After Mary Hilson, the Nordic attitudes are quite similar, Scandinavians also appreciate such values. The huge difference between these nations is that, in contrary to Scandinavian people, Americans consider the state as evil. It is often seen as a natural enemy and the less the government knows about you, so much the better. Americans are nearly scared of the thought lying too heavily on support. For this reason, the USA are located in the lowest category of the *Three Worlds of Welfare Capitalism* instead, like the Nordic countries, in the highest one.

For me it is remarkable that the citizens of two nations have nearly the same strong basic values yet the relationship between the state and its inhibits is such a pivotal factor that it decides which system rules the country.

III – 21.9.2010: Nordic cultural identity

One central feature of the Nordic cultural identity is definitely *Lutheranism*. The Lutheran reformation in the 16th century created a strong *state church*, thus a church which worked together with the state. This rare happening was due to the fact that the reformation had been a state-driven project, so that the king could gain power at the expense of the church.

This was not the only aim the government had. It wanted to keep the homogeneity in society, no other protestant movements should occur. Moreover, a reformation imposed from above strengthens the connection to the state. The third reason dealt with controlling the people. The First Communion for instance could now be used as a border at which one receives the status of an adult and get the permission for marriage. In addition, the confession often had been made collective and in public and the people's reading skills were tested. So the church became an instrument for controlling and administration.

When the Lutheran church got restructured during the reformation the scholastic method had been one point of criticism. It was claimed that one should rely again on the original texts in the bible, mostly on the New Testament. Furthermore, the priesthood was made less exclusive so that the sermons and the preaching stayed focussed. Nonetheless, the priest stayed the central figure in church. He needed to combine the church's as well as the state's task so he taught the citizens about religion while being also some kind of information channel for authorities.

After Henrik Stenius the Lutheran culture had an impact on how Nordic, modern societies were built. Indeed, there is a link between Lutheranism and the Welfare State. It is a connection between a pre-modern society and a modern one which is characterized by the strong belief in the model of the Good State. Working is also one of these junctures; it is the personal involvement in society. You need to work to be an active part of this society.

Nowadays the state has undertaken the church's tasks. It does not matter in which field a problem occurs, the citizen always can turn to the state. This potent relationship between state and individual advances individualism, freedom, a desired loneliness, and conformity.

I was surprised when I read Henrik Stenius' text about Lutheran tradition in which it was said that the Lutheran reformation had been state-driven. No other country comes to my mind where a reformation was not accomplished by unsatisfied citizens. I really appreciate this Nordic handling because in my opinion it is very important to have a good bond between church and state. You often get to hear that church and state, probably the two most important executives in every country, quarrel about more or less significant topics. This causes disturbance among the citizens and exacerbates being a unity. So the best solution is church and state working hand in hand.

IV – 23.9.2010: Nordic housing - building modernity

Architectural work in Finland and Sweden has been a central aspect of politics from the 1930s until the 1950s. *Functionalism* became the dominant building style which followed the slogan *less is more*. There should be a strict break with the old bourgeoisie, so ornaments were definitely no feature of the functionalism. Instead there were minimalism, lighting, and bright colours. Rooms and furniture needed to have a simple design so that the form could follow the function. Three keywords influenced this architecture the most: hygiene, rationality and practicality.

Renewing the housing situation was not the primary aim of this state-driven project. It should be just one step to a higher goal, namely to create a new and better society. The idea of an expert-society was very strong, therefore, a proper and clean environment needed to be created for the children. Furthermore, the new dwellings should represent this raising of the better society. They became a visible symbol of modernity.

Alva and Gunnar Myrdal were central actors in the Nordic movement of functionalism. They campaigned for better housing situations, a proper education and family planning. Their aim was to build habitations for mass society. In Sweden 1936, the *Barnrikehus* or *Myrdalshus* was invented. These houses were especially constructed for large and poor families in which they could live on 50-60 m². Another project of the Myrdal's was the *Kollektivhus* or also called *service flat*. In these habitations housework and childcare were collectivized so that both father and mother could work outside the home.

In all these new dwellings there were several advantages in comparison with the former flats people had to live in. Central heating, bright colours, a bathroom and collective rooms are some of them but also the new division of space played a big role. The kitchen and the living room got separated since the kitchen grew more and more important. When domestic work had been accepted as some kind of real work there was even scientific research on practicality and effectiveness in housekeeping. The housewife's work should be as easy as possible.

Functionalism was imposed from above, the architecture had been the state's task. It was promoted as a part of the national popular culture heritage, nevertheless there were strong debates and conflicts about it. That the state wanted to shape not just the modern home but also the people's way of life was not accepted in every mind. So it is no surprise that there was not only functionalism during this period of time. In the 1970s for example also rural romanticism took place which preferred dark colours. Today functionalism has its comeback in Finland. The significant simplicity and the diffusion of minimalist design are reflected in *neo-functionalism*. Nowadays this is no more a state-driven project, rather pivotal are town-planning and aesthetic reasons.

When this lesson about Nordic housing and the functionalism ended and I walked home, I paid attention to the architecture style of the city-centre. Most of the buildings have copious ornaments and are designed elaborately. I turned in some side streets and again I looked at houses which were decorated with pillars or mouldings. I thought of the university, the cathedral or the train station, none of them have any features of minimalism architecture.

So where are all these buildings that had been influenced by the functionalism? I did some research on this and I got to know that an architect designed the city-centre along the lines of Saint Petersburg after Helsinki was named to the capital of Finland. Since then this town is known as a stronghold of *classicism*. This classicism is reflected for example in the university building and the cathedral. Another strong influence had been the *art nouveau*, the train station had been designed in this style.

Finally I found some popular buildings arisen during functionalism, for instance the Olympic stadium in Töölö and the Finlandia-Hall near Töölönlahti. At least I even discovered that the cultural centre *Lasipalatsi*, which I pass almost every day, is one of the functionalist constructions. I will take a closer look next time I walk by.

V – 28.9.2010: Alcohol in Nordic societies

Before I came to Finland for the first time I thought about things that I associate with this country. The strongest ideas were the beautiful landscape, a quite difficult language, a superior education system – and alcohol problems. Some images one has about a certain country might be prejudices, so I tried to stay as neutral as I could when I arrived in Helsinki.

Yet already on my early days I made my first experience with a drunkard. It was a sunny, warm day when I was on my way home and discovered this man lying on a grass field between two streets. At first I thought he needs some help but everybody just passed and ignored him. So it became clear to me that the man must simply sleep off until he was sober. A few days later I made a similar experience when I did not pay attention and nearly stumbled over a drunken man lying at the harbour basin. These two examples may be coincidences and are of course not representative for a whole society. Yet another incident also confirmed my concerns about how Fins handle alcohol. In the train station there is a small bar I pass every time I go to university. There are always people in it, people of every age and gender. I even saw men in suits drinking their first beer at half past eight in the morning.

So I was really looking forward to our seventh lecture that dealt with the topic *Alcohol in Nordic societies*. I learned that alcohol is indeed a social problem or maybe also the other way around: alcohol might be the consequence of social problems. A good proof of this statement is the pure alcohol consumption per inhabitant: 12.5 litres. Nevertheless, this is not the top of the ranking in Europe. I have found out that for example Luxembourg has a consumption about 15.6 litres per inhabitant and that my home country Germany has got nearly the same figure as the Nordic states (12 litres/inhabitant).

There are mainly two reasons why the alcohol consumption in the Nordic states is so high. At first, there are of course economical reasons. The state can easily earn money with this business. The second one lies in the cultural history. Alcohol has never been in a category of nutrition, it was rather a symbol of luxury. Moreover, alcohol is considered as one fixed part of having fun. When people go out for a party one aim is to get drunk. Almost nobody is abstinent because alcohol is present everywhere. Only five to ten percent of the population never drinks any alcohol. Young Finnish people are indeed told to not start too early with drinking but this has nearly no effect. Alcohol education is not very common as well, reportedly it should be a waste of effort.

There are some serious consequences due to this handling. Finland for instance is one of the safest countries in Europe but on the other hand the violent crimes which happen nonetheless are often alcohol-related. I have read an interesting article a few days ago with which I want to confirm this relation between alcohol and violence. In the 1920s there had been a period when the murder rate was three times higher than today. More than forty years later, in 1969, another wave of murder arrived because it hat been legalized to sell beer in retail industry. Another increase of violence had been noticed when alcohol taxes were reduced in 2004.

So the death rate needs follows the total alcohol consumption. In 2005, the most common cause of death among working people has been alcohol.

There is a long history of alcohol policy in the Nordic states which can be divided into five time periods.

1. **1850 – 1910:** At first, alcohol has been a moral question in the poor, new rising nations. Drinking was mainly male and with the aim for intoxication.

2. **1910 – 1930s:** During this time period there are the first prohibitions of alcohol. Local moderations were imposed and laws dealing with public drunkenness were sharpened. Despite these measures the number of drunkards increased since an extensive black market has developed. In 1932, prohibitions ended.

3. **1945 – 1970:** After World War II the alcohol consumption has been relative low. People were just too poor to buy lots of alcohol. In addition, the alcohol taxes raised which have become an important source of the states' revenues.

4. **1970 – 1990:** Alcohol grew more important again and several theories about the total consumption appeared. Drinking had been seen as a collective phenomenon everybody takes part in. To gain some control of the situation new laws were established. People's social rights could be limited if they were drunkards, for example they were not allowed to vote anymore.

5. **1990 - Today:** Meanwhile, there is a new alcohol economy which follows the slogan *less state, more market.*

VI – 7.10.2010: Nordic democracy

There are lots of different democratic models in the politic world, for instance the French revolutionary democracy, the American democracy, and the British parliamentarism. So what means Nordic democracy?

Many topics are closely linked to this question. It refers for example to a long history of peace and freedom. Nordic peasants never had to bear feudalism, they lived free and under their own control. Yet also anti-power politics contributed to the image of Nordic democracy. The attitude of neutrality the Nordic states kept up during the Cold War between Western world and Eastern world from 1945 up to the 1980s made them some kind of experts in solving conflicts. When the Cold War was finally over democracy had won. Yet which one? Eastern and Western bloc had different opinions about democracy, so the Nordic one was somehow a middle way between both.

Another point is the high gender equality. Lots of women participate in the labour market and in politics, although the labour market is still gender-divided. Nevertheless, the gender equality is an important part of the Nordic democracy.

The Welfare State has the strongest connection to Nordic democracy. This middle way between socialism and capitalism has even become nearly synonymous for Nordic democracy nowadays.

This type of Scandinavian democracy has proofed its benefit not only during the Cold War but already during the 1930s. The Nordic States, Finland at this point of time not included yet, have been the calming democratic influence in this period of totalitarianism. Instead of also sliding in this totalitarianism they formed their nationality by combining universalism with particularism – without being too national. Maybe things like adult education, the social security or just the long years of self-government prevented the Nordic states from the idea of totalitarianism.

From the 1980s up to 2000, there was a significant change in Nordic democracy. The Welfare State grew more and more important and, as I already mentioned, it became synonymous for Nordic democracy. Moreover, this system got challenged by other European models, so it needed to be defended.

I really appreciate the Nordic system of democracy and the Welfare State model. It is special to have such a peaceful national history which even survived both World Wars. It is not just their neutrality, the states have even gone further and tried to interfere in the Cold War which is commendable.

My home country Germany is probably the total opposite of the Scandinavian states. It has been responsible for World War II and was also blamed for the First World War, so peace is definitely a missing feature in German history. I regret this because even if neither me nor my parents have lived in any of those times, one is still confronted with these things. You cannot avoid the history of your home country. Sometimes it is the first topic that comes to the people's mind when they think about a certain state.

Of course the size of the country plays an important role when talking about leading wars. The Nordic states maybe had not enough military power to challenge other countries and they were just too small to have high-flying visions. Nevertheless, I do not believe that this is the explanation for the peaceful history. The state's condition cannot be the only reason for this.

However, I really wish that I would live in a country with such a non-violent past. I like the neutrality the Nordic states tried to keep up during every period of time where other countries slid into destroying combats.

VII – 12.10.2010: Scandinavian sin

The idea of a frivolity in sexual matters in Scandinavia, especially in Sweden, is often associated by foreigners. Also coldness and unromantic behaviour are frequently in the people's mind concerning the Nordic love life. *Susan Sontag* described these contradictory aspects – sexual liberty versus rational control – in a letter in which she declared a deep fear of conflicts as the cause for the Swedish liberalism. However, another person who studied the Nordic way of life as well, *Roland Huntford*, came to the conclusion that Swedes believed if they were sexually emancipated it meant they were also free individuals.

How has this sexual liberalism actually developed?

Many topics which would be handled private or among the citizens in other countries are the state's tasks in the Nordic countries, for instance the housing question and the church reformation. Like these, sexuality and enlightenment were political themes in Scandinavia, too. The state had an interest in the nation's reproduction to retain it whereas both quality and quantity counted. For this, economic security needed to be provided so that people feel safe and could concentrate on family planning. Furthermore, medical science and other political decisions had to enable the intention. Sexual education has been made a part of the curriculum in school.

People like Elise Ottesen-Jensen belonged to the avant-garde in matters concerning enlightenment and sexuality in the Nordic regions. For her, sexuality should be an expression of intimacy, joy and tenderness. In 1933, she founded the *Riksförbundet för Sexuell Upplysning* (RFSU) which is still active today. In the beginnings, this association was not supported by the state. Just in the fifties and sixties it became a part of the government's policy. In the focus of the government were married couples and families. Since the eighties the youth also moved into focus.

I already mentioned above that the church reformation was indicated by the state, so state and church were normally working together. Yet in this sexuality-question the Lutheran church had a different opinion than the state. Nevertheless, it was more or less forced to accept the strategy the government had pursued.

The notion of *Swedish sin* became famous especially through films. A direct impact on liberalism had for example the film *Hon dansade en sommar* (One summer of Happiness) shown in 1951. It contained the first nude scene in art cinema and tended to break with the old order. In some countries this film was even forbidden, like in Norway. Eighteen years later, in 1969, a new, disputed film came onto the market. *Kärlekens språk* (Language of Love) was an educational movie including an expert panel commenting on the happening. The film had the intention to be a serious project which involved besides these professionals also statistics and scientific explanations. All in all, it needed to be seen as a radical attack on taboos concerning sexuality. Of course offensives like this one caused protests in other nations. In London 30.000 people demonstrated against this film and probably not only against this film but also against the handling of sexuality in Scandinavia in general. It was not accepted that a nation perceived sexuality as a part of living as a modern and normal human being.

Nowadays, this image of the *Scandinavian sin* is not as strong as in the past anymore. I even have to admit that I have never heard of it before. Sexuality and liberalism were definitely no features I associated with the Nordic countries. Nonetheless, after living in Helsinki for several weeks, I can confirm that Fins use to be more permissive in relation to nudity than perhaps other nations are.

One time I went swimming and I was a little bit confused when I entered the women's changing room. In Germany we have small changing rooms for single persons where everyone has his or her privacy. However, in this Finnish swimming bath there was only one huge, collective changing room. Nude women crossed the room to get downstairs to the showers and to the sauna and they did not use a towel or something like that to cover anything. Before I went downstairs I discovered a sign which asked to take the shower without swimwear. Obviously it was no problem for any of the other women to be naked, they seemed to feel comfortable. Yet I noticed that some kind of inhibitions rose in my mind because the Western part of Germany is not very permissive. Apparently, the society I grew up in is not as libertine as the Finnish one.

VIII – 14.10.2010: Voices of immigration

1.9 % of the Finnish people were born abroad – this is a very low rate. In Helsinki there is a percentage of foreigners of 10, nevertheless this is still low. Finnish emigration outnumbered the immigration in the 1980s, in Denmark, Sweden, and Norway it had been already outnumbered in the 1930s. Just in the seventies (Denmark, Sweden, Norway) and in the nineties (Finland) refugees and asylum seekers arrived.

Multiculturalism seems to be a difficult topic in Scandinavia. In former times people used to want to have multiculturalism, however, they preferred not to live in it. A paradox example for this attitude are international schools. Many parents would like to send their children to an international school yet in this school the percentage of foreigners may not be too high. Nowadays, the citizen's desires have changed – people do not only refuse to live in a multicultural society but also do not want to *have* any.

Most of this lecture was about literature that deals with the topic immigration. The authors, so-called *immigrant authors*, are people who immigrated to Finland and wrote about their experiences in the new country. The first books being published on this topic consisted of different reports about persons who emigrated and their first impressions.

From 1970 until the year 2000 there were some topics which were used by nearly all of these immigrant authors. Homesickness, rootlessness, and the feeling of being *in between* (two countries, two cultures, etc.) were some guiding themes. The stories often were a mixture of the old and the new place of living whereas the old one could also be criticized. Yet the focus lay on the present life of the immigrants and not on their former one.

A typical plot could have been for instance an intercultural encounter; a love story between a woman and a man, a violent clash but also a humorous and self-ironic narration. The protagonists were mostly from the working class, for example a cleaner. The welfare state could also play a role.

In the year 2000 there was finally a significant change in this field of literature. Suddenly there was more interest in authors who tell their immigration stories. They got national attention and were welcomed with open arms to talk about their experiences. By this time the term *immigrant author* was still in use. Many authors were very frustrated to be classified like this because they were born in the state they lived in, only their parents or one parent had immigrated. Nevertheless, most of these authors wrote about topics which were connected to multiculturalism.

There were some noteworthy authors who wrote their books in this period of time. The Swede *Alejandro Leiva Wenger* for instance tricked his reader by writing the first two chapters in incorrect Swedish language and started just later on with talking in a proper, formal way. *Jonas Hassen Khemiri* wrote one of the most sold books in Sweden called *Ett öga rött*. Together with Wenger and another author, *Johannes Anguru*, he visited many TV shows and was in a great demand.

The first woman getting attention in Sweden through her novel was *Marjaneh Bakhtiari*. In her story she let the characters talk about immigration and multiculturalism, each of them from a different point of view. Bakhtiari called her book *Kalla det vad fan du vill* in the knowledge that she too would be classified as an immigrant author. Like her, *Ranya Paasonen* was also very frustrated about being in this category. She did not tell her own story but the one of her parents.

In all these books about immigration language is an important feature. The writers created some new type of language which was of course not because of poor language acquisitions. By using a wrong word order or by borrowing words from a foreign language (often Turkish) they took advantage of the linguistic creativity.

I was a little bit disappointed of this lecture. I imagined we would talk about questions like *where do the immigrants in the Nordic countries come from, why is there such a low rate of people being born abroad* and *what do laws say about immigration*. Talking about literature that deals with multiculturalism was not very interesting for me, especially because we did not go in detail of any of the presented novels.

Nonetheless, it is good to know that in the last decade there had been such a sensation in Scandinavia (mainly Sweden) about these immigrant authors.

YOUR KNOWLEDGE HAS VALUE

- We will publish your bachelor's and
  master's thesis, essays and papers

- Your own eBook and book -
  sold worldwide in all relevant shops

- Earn money with each sale

Upload your text at www.GRIN.com
and publish for free